IN THE GARDEN WITH MY LORD

KATHI OWENS

BookLeaf Publishing

India | USA | UK

Presentation by *BookLeaf Publishing*

Web: www.bookleafpub.com

E-mail: info@bookleafpub.com

ISBN: 9789360948047

First edition 2024

I dedicate this book to my Lord and Savior Jesus Christ. He has given me the heart and the ability to write. And to the Holy Spirit, who opened my eyes to the truth of His word. I pray that my writing brings glory to God, for He is worthy of all.

And to those who preach and teach His truths and doctrines, I dedicate this book, especially to my husband and former pastor, Al Owens, I love you!

ACKNOWLEDGEMENT

All Scriptures quotations are taken from the King James Version (KJV)--Public Domain

My English teacher at Notre Dame High School in Portsmouth, Ohio, Sister Ingrid, was creative in developing a love of writing in her students. Studying the writing forms of various poets, both classical as well as the popular poets of the day, she assigned writing in multiple styles and subjects. I attribute my love of writing and reading poetry to her teaching.

PREFACE

Every person is endowed with some skill or talent that may be used to honor our Creator and God. The Lord has given me the skill and desire to write. The poetry in my book is primarily about my Lord and Savior, Jesus. He has been merciful to me, has saved me and forgiven me, and is preparing a place for me to live eternally with Him in Heaven. My prayer is that all who read this book know Him and love Him as I do.

Call to Him

Psalm 107:13 "Then they cried unto the LORD in their trouble, and he saved them out of their distresses."

Call unto Jesus in your times of trouble:
In your loneliness He will give you love;
In your chaos He will give you peace;
In your danger He will give you safety;
In your confusion He will give you understanding;
In your sickness He will give you healing;
In your sorrow He will give you comfort;
In your guilt He will give you forgiveness.

Call to Jesus, He will hear, He will answer. He is always near.

Judge Not

Matthew 7:1 "Judge not, that ye be not judged."

Look at him, I say,
How he acts day by day.
He's so obsessed with want and need;
He is consumed by desire and greed.
He misses church week after week,
And praise from others is what he seeks.

Look at her, I say,
How she acts day by day.
She runs around with gossip and dirt,
The tales she spreads bring shame and hurt.
Her children are wild, and stingy, and mean.
She's a poor mother, it's easily seen.

Then I looked and I saw me,
And what kind of person did I see?
One who knows the Lord's mercy and grace,
And suddenly I felt tremendous disgrace.
For I'd not invited him to Sunday service;
My friendliness to him was hit and miss.
I listened to her critical tales
And added my take of how she fails.
But never did I offer a hand

With her little brood and all it demands.

Then I prayed, Lord forgive me, help me
improve,
Help me to be a Christian whose actions you
approve.
Help me be loving and righteous and kind,
In others their goodness and character find,
To share with others your care and your grace
And remove my opinions and with love replace.

The Faithful One

Lamentations 3:22-23 "It is of the LORD's
mercies that we are not consumed, because his
compassions fail not. They are new every
morning: great is thy faithfulness."

Who can know One so faithful?
He is there for me morning and night.
He provides strength and comfort in trials,
In the darkest of days shines His light.

When my very best friend has betrayed me;
When all of my efforts have failed
He tells me sweetly, as He holds me close,
For you to the cross I was nailed.

He reminds me of the pain He has suffered,
How He's preparing a mansion for me.
This life, like a breath, is soon over
And in glory with Him I will be.

Then my heart fills with love and with wonder
That Jesus my God and my Friend
Is there to uplift and to cheer me.
He promises to be near till the end.

Beauty

Proverbs 31:30 "Favour is deceitful, and beauty
is vain: but a woman that feareth the LORD, she
shall be praised."

The beauty of youth is slipping away;
Tight strong muscles are now soft today.

My skin's lost its glow, now there's spots and
baggin'
The firmness I had, now all is a saggin'!

Exercise and aerobics used to firm up the
waistline;
Feels all that I do now just wastes my time.

Every half ounce of delight seems to add on a
pound,
Where I had curves and shape, I am now pudgy
and round.

The one thing I pray as I age and grow older:
That with each passing day, my faith becomes
bolder.

That the beauty without will be replaced with a
new
Beauty within and with wisdom too.

What a trade that would be--to lose outward
beauty
To gain love for others and to fulfill Godly duty.

Perhaps then instead of seeing grey hair,
My friends will see Jesus in the smile that I
wear.

Instead of them seeing what time's done to my
skin,
They will see God's love and strength that's
within.

For the beauty inside never fades away,
It endures till that time that I join Jesus some
day!

Behold the Lamb of God!

John 1:29 "The next day John seeth Jesus
coming unto him, and saith, Behold the Lamb of
God, which taketh away the sin of the world."

John the Baptist prepared the way
For the Man Jesus Christ,
The promised Messiah, Lord, and King,
Declaring, "Behold the Lamb of God".

As those who leave this world
Who know Christ as their Lord,
Upon entering Heaven's gates,
Do they hear, "Behold the Lamb of God"?

One day I will go through those pearly gates,
And many loved ones see--
But what I want most
Is to behold the Lamb of God!

And one day that trump will sound
As Jesus Christ returns.
As every eye views Him,
Will we hear again, "Behold the Lamb of God"?

God Speaks

Ezekiel 12:25 "For I am the Lord: I will speak,
and the word that I shall speak shall come to
pass…"

The Lord spoke to Adam in the garden.
He instructed Noah to build the ark.
He told Jonah to go to Ninevah;
And told Abraham about the stars.

God called to Moses from the burning bush,
He spoke to Samuel as he lay in bed;
He talked to David through the man Nathan,
And to Daniel he told of things to come.

He called to Jacob in a dream as he slept;
He told Joshua to go over Jordan.
He gave Joseph dream explanations.
He told Gideon how to free Israel from
oppression.

Our Lord talked to prophets and leaders and
kings;
He spoke to the apostles too.
His voice was heard when John baptized Jesus,
And He spoke to Paul on the road to Damascus.

God speaks to me, as I read His word,
He shows me His wonderful works.
He tells of His promises of the glories of
Heaven;
And a place where I will never grow old.

Do you want to hear our Lord speak to you?
His word was written for us.
His truths are recorded and saved for all time,
That we might know Him and His will.

On to Heaven

When I have gone
And departed from this earth,
Rejoice with me,
For I've had a second birth!

Don't cry due to death,
But celebrate with me--
For I've gone to be with Jesus
To the place I've longed to be.

I've received now my crown
I've seen the Lord's blessed face;
Now departed from this wicked world
I'm now in the perfect place.

My mansion's standing ready.
There is no sorrow here.
I'm just thanking my Lord Jesus,
Along with many I love so dear.

So as my body is lowered
Into that cold grave in the earth,
Rejoice along with me
For I've had a second birth!

Seasons of Life

Ecclesiastes 3:1 "To every thing there is a season, and a time to every purpose under the heaven."

The springtime is a carefree season,
Full of laughter, lighthearted life.
Breezes bring a cheery song;
No signs of toil, no signs of strife.

The summer comes with warm pleasures.
Friendships grow in the sunlit days.
All around is frolicking and fun
As at the beautiful sunsets we gaze.

The fall arrives with a cool wind:
The splendor of color covers the hilltops.
God's provision is seen in the harvest,
Days spent toiling and gathering crops.

Then winter brings the coldness of death
Of living things bright and green.
Also enters peace and silence
And remembrance of the past we've seen.

Alas, springtime breaks again!

New life returns, bursting forth from the ground.
God is in control, all time is His--
Let us give praise and make a joyful sound!

The Sewing Room

The sewing room is my haven for thinking,
The place where I can slip away.
And while cutting and marking and making
Sleeves and cuffs and facings
I escape today and travel to other places, other
times.

As the zipper I stitch into a skirt,
I may be reliving some past moment in my
mind.
Or I might be solving problems with
My children or in the world,
As I press and sew the hems upon my slacks.

As I assemble a blouse or a jacket,
I may be in the time machine in my thoughts:
In future moments or days or months or years
Dreaming of what may one day happen,
As the sewing machine hums its little tune.

One thing you can be sure of,
When you see me stitching steadily--
I really am not there at all in mind,
I have gone on a leave of absence
When I sew and stitch away.

The Betrayer

Matthew 26:49-50 "And forthwith he came to
Jesus, and said, Hail, master, and kissed him.
And Jesus said unto him, Friend, wherefore art
thou come? Then came they, and laid hands on
Jesus and took him."

That friend: so dear and trusted,
Confidences shared;
Supped together, traveled together--
That friend.

That friend: gifts given, so loved,
Memories of precious hours,
Laughter, tears, hugs, kisses--
That friend.

That friend: lied, betrayed,
Like an asp, cold and bitter,
Turned away without acknowledgement--
That friend.

Words, O How I Love Words

Jeremiah 15:16 "Thy words were found, and I
did eat them;
and thy word was unto me the joy and rejoicing
of mine heart:
for I am called by thy name, O LORD God of
hosts."

Words, oh how I love to read them,
Words, how I love to write!
I love to study and sing them,
I love them day and night!

I must search out their meaning.
I use them every day.
Words are in my every thought,
And in everything I say.

I read the words in books,
I read them in the paper.
I read the words on cereal boxes,
And those written on notepaper.

I found the precious words of God
When I was just a teen.
Those words of life I love so much

Caused my soul to be washed clean.

Those words of Scripture written,
Of God and His Begotten Son
Showed me my sin and need of Christ,
That on the cross my salvation won.

I love to read of my Savior
Of His mercy and love for me.
I write that others may also believe
And that their souls may be set free.

You are Here, Lord

Psalm 125:2 "As the mountains are round about
Jerusalem, so the LORD is round about his
people from henceforth even for ever."

Lord, you're all about me in this world,
In so many forms you are there.
Your power is shown in the mountains
And your strength rolls on the waves of the sea.

Your voice is heard in the booming thunder,
Your majesty is written in the stars.
Your greatness walks throughout the forest,
And your far-reaching hand is in the desert.

The canyons echo your wonderful name,
The clear blue sky tells of your eternity.
The lightening displays your might and glory
And the rainbow speaks of your grace.

The whole earth shouts with your being
And reveals your breathtaking beauty;
Your soft hand touches creation with a breeze
And the sunlight transfers the warmth of your
love.

Your Spirit travels from horizon to horizon;
You are here Lord upon this land.
Your tender care is evident all about me;
You are here Lord upon this land.

God's Word

Is a hammer to break the heart of stone
Is a sword of the Spirit of God
Is a light for the way
Is a lamp for the feet
Is a map for direction
Is an instruction book for life
Is a seed to grow spiritual fruit
Is water to wash away the filthiness of sin
Is a fire burning within
Is the rule for a happy life
Is food for the hungry
Is a purifier of the defiled.

It endures
It is sure
It is inspired
It is purposeful
It is perfect
It is powerful
It is pure
It is sacred
It is fulfilled
It is holy
It is a standard to live by
It is kept in the heart of the believer

It contains secrets revealed to those who seek

It is searched
It is spoken
It is studied
It is taught
It is read
It is loved
It instructs
It reproves
It inspires
It comforts
It brings joy unspeakable
It gives hope not understandable
It tells of a future unimaginable

It is despised by Satan and his followers
It is loved by those who love God!

Strength for the Battle

Exodus 19:4 "...I bare you on eagles' wings, and
brought you unto myself."

Be with me Lord in trials
When the enemy is strong;
Your strength is sufficient
When the battle is long.

Lift me up on eagles' wings
Show me your great power.
Let me draw from your strength
In my weakest hour.

I am as one with no strength,
Victory is only in You.
I rest upon your bosom,
Your word, oh God, is true.

Before the world I'm nothing;
To You I give all glory,
To all I will proclaim
Jesus Christ, His wondrous story.

And when before the enemy
I stand to begin the fight,

You are there beside me, Lord,
And in each victory I'll delight.

For your strength is unending,
And your might is forever;
And when I look to You for power
You will forsake me never.

The Bread of Life is Received

As I daily open thy word, O Lord,
I pray for blessings from the reading--
That You will give to me what you have
And You will apply it as You will.

You give comfort in your word
And wisdom from your Scriptures.
You gave salvation many years ago
And give strength with each passing day.

Words of mercy, love, and grace,
Words to cheer and encourage;
Words that instill bravery to stand
And power to overcome temptations to sin;

Writings of hope for a better day
When You return to take me home;
Of eternity sharing your glory
When sin and Satan will be no more.

In Whose Hands is your Life?

Your life, so precious,
You place in others' hands:
The physician and surgeon,
The bus driver and airline pilot,
The ones who assemble your vehicle,
The ones who fit together the amusement park
ride,
The relative or friend who drives you home.
That life is only the physical life, the life you
know will end.

Your life, your eternal soul,
In whose hands do you place?
You seek riches and power,
You search for love and passion,
You travel the world,
You lock yourself in your abode,
You serve others to bring self-satisfaction.
That eternal life is the life that continues after
the body is dead and decayed.

You have taken your life into your own hands:
Seeking love,
Seeking consent,

Seeking friendship,
Seeking for tunes,
Forever seeking happiness.
Joyfulness found for a moment, a day, a week,
or a year.
Not true and forever happiness.

Place your life into the hand of Jesus, where you
will find:
Happiness,
Peace,
Love,
Riches,
Friendship,
Acceptance,
Mercy, and Grace,
And an eternity in His glorious presence.

Redemption Draweth Nigh

Luke 21:27-28 "And then shall they see the Son of man coming in a cloud with power and great glory. And when these things begin to come to pass, then look up, and lift up your heads; for your redemption draweth nigh."

Jesus came to earth to save
A people dying and lost.
Born as a babe, He grew and aged,
He knew what would be the cost.

He healed the sick and raised the dead,
He taught of God His Father.
He was spat upon, mocked, and tried,
His death witnessed by His mother.

He told His disciples this was coming:
His horrible death on a tree,
But on the third day He would rise
To reign eternally.

He'll come again as He said
In power and great glory.
Look to the eastern sky He says,
This was His oratory.

Lift up your heads He exclaimed,
Your redemption draweth nigh.
Then one day in Heaven He'll be
Lifted up on high.

He'll sit on the Father's own right hand,
He'll reign as King of Kings.
The saints and angels round Him gather,
And many praises to Him they'll sing.

He is worthy of your praise and worship,
He is deserving of your love.
If you repent and turn to Him,
You'll reign with Him above.

To My Children

If we could, when we leave, give our children,
Not the riches and money we've earned,
But those many things most important in life:
Wisdom and the things that we've learned.

To call on the Lord in time of great trial,
To thank Him for many blessings bestowed;
To ask Him for guidance and safety each day,
To lead us at every crossroad.

For His comfort and love, to be thankful too,
Share His blessings with others we know.
Give others encouragement, be faithful to Him,
And to those less fortunate, let kindness show.

Tell others of Jesus, of His life and His death,
Tell the wonderful works you have heard.
Give much to the Lord, He'll return to you
greatly,
This promise He gave in His word.

Don't depend upon people for happiness and joy.
Man is sinful, unfaithful, untrue.
Friends will disappoint you each turn of the
way--

Let God's word tell you just what to do.

Look to Jesus for comfort and guidance and
love;
And if you live for Jesus only each day
In your life you'll be happy, you'll have joy,
peace, and hope,
And far from Him He won't let you stray.

So children, you'll have whatever is mine,
When I'm gone and you're left alone.
But search in His word, find His truth for
yourself,
For what I know, you find in Jesus alone.

Appalacian Springtime

The glow of the moonlight demands a hush in
the land.
Only crickets and tree frogs sing their lullaby.
The soft breeze sweeps away the cares of the
day,
Twinkling stars speak out, "No worries".

Not a human sound is heard.
The dogs content to sleep in their houses,
Coyotes and owls nap in the silence.
Even the felines are dozing and quiet.

The only sound is that still small voice,
God telling me of His grace and mercy.
As the light wind wraps His loving arms around
me
He tells me all is well, He is here.

The Sunday School Teacher

1 Corinthians 15:58 "...be ye stedfast,
unmoveable, always abounding in the work of
the Lord, forasmuch as ye know that your labour
is not in vain in the Lord."

When you see their little faces
Change and mature as seasons pass,
You remember when you taught them
In your Sunday School Class.

When you see them stand before the church
To sing a hymn of praise;
When a young man brings devotion,
And he speaks of better days.

When a young one comes before the church
Professing Christ as Lord;
When one recites from memory
Sweet verses from His word.

Your heart swells up within you,
You see God's work within this child,
And you know the Lord has used your voice,
And each lesson was worthwhile.

And as you teach the different children,
You see them grow as seasons pass,
Be sure to teach them truth and love
In your Sunday School Class.

A Poem of Worship

Jude 25 "To the only wise God our Saviour, be
glory and majesty, dominion and power, both
now and ever. Amen."

I glorify and worship you,
Who in your majesty reigns Supreme.
Your power is awesome.
Your glory is wondrous;
Your dominion is infinite.

I glorify and worship you,
Who rules with might and strength.
Your beauty is unspeakable,
Your knowledge is beyond understanding,
Your judgment is justice.

I glorify and worship you,
Who extends mercy and forgiveness.
Your love is immeasurable,
Your compassion is unbounded,
Your grace is everlasting.

I glorify and worship you alone, O my God!